Janek Dyer

NURSERY RHYMES AND SONGS FROM
LISTEN WITH MOTHER

NURSERY RHYMES AND SONGS FROM

LISTEN
WITH MOTHER

Compiled by Valerie McCarthy

Illustrated by Douglas Hall

Published in association
with the BBC

HUTCHINSON
London Melbourne Sydney Auckland Johannesburg

Hutchinson Children's Books Ltd

An imprint of the Hutchinson Publishing Group

17–21 Conway Street, London W1P 6JD

Hutchinson Publishing Group Australia Pty Ltd
PO Box 496, 16–22 Church Street, Hawthorne, Melbourne, Victoria 3122

Hutchinson Group (NZ) Ltd
32–34 View Road, PO Box 40-086, Glenfield, Auckland 10

Hutchinson Group (SA) Pty Ltd
PO Box 337, Bergvlei 2012, South Africa

First published 1984

Illustrations © Douglas Hall 1984

Set in Plantin

Printed and bound in Great Britain by
Anchor Brendon Ltd, Tiptree, Essex

ISBN 0 09 158640 2

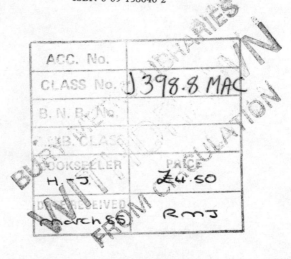

Contents

The Cat and the Fiddle

Things We Do

We'll All Have Tea

Those Funny People

Acknowledgements

The compiler and publisher wish to thank the following for permission to use copyright material in this collection:

Chantelle Music Ltd for 'The Hippopotamus Lullabye', 'Charlotte's Navy Blue Shoes' by Nola York; 'The Fish in the Pond', 'Samantha the Panther', 'I Am Mixing Colours', 'Tearing Paper', 'Walking in the Garden' by Michael Richmond and Nola York, and 'Follow My Leader' by Jenyth Worsley.
Ward Lock Educational Ltd for 'The Funny Family', 'We're Going on a Bearhunt', and 'I Have a Bonnet Trimmed With Blue' from *The Funny Family* compiled by Alison McMorland.

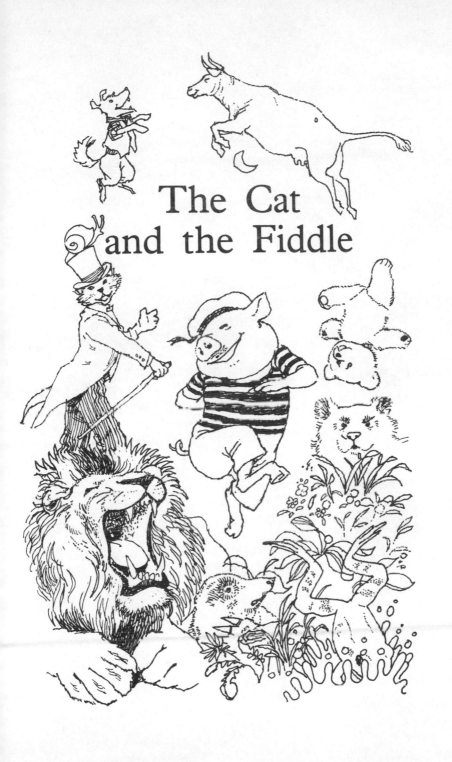

The Cat
and the Fiddle

The Octopus

It's quite a lengthy business,
When an octopus gets dressed.
He likes his trousers ironed,
He likes them cleaned and pressed.
And dressing for an octopus,
Is not a lot of fun:
There's eight black socks and eight black shoes,
And laces to be done!

Clive Riche

Fernando the Frog

Fernando the frog,
Lives in a bog,
And he loves the thunder and the rain.
He jumps into puddles,
    Jump hands forwards.
And splashes and paddles,
And then he jumps out again!
    Jump hands backwards.

Valerie McCarthy

Pussycat

Pussycat, Pussycat,
Where have you been?
I've been to London,
To visit the Queen.

Pussycat, Pussycat,
What did you there?
I frightened a little mouse
Under the chair.

Traditional

Slowly, Slowly

Slowly, slowly, very slowly
Creeps the garden snail,
Slowly, slowly, very slowly
Up the wooden rail.

Quickly, quickly, very quickly,
Runs the little mouse,
Quickly, quickly, very quickly
Round about the house.

Traditional

Little Piggy

Where are you going, you little pig?
I'm leaving my mother, I'm growing so big!
  So big, so big!
  So young, so big!
What leaving your mother, you foolish young pig?

Where are you going, you little pig?
I've got a new spade, and I'm going to dig!
  To dig, little pig!
  A little pig dig!
Well, I never saw a pig with a spade that could dig!

Where are you going, you little pig?
Why, I'm going to have a nice ride in a gig!
  In a gig, little pig!
  What, a pig in a gig!
Well, I never yet saw a pig in a gig!

Where are you going, you little pig?
I'm going to the barber's to buy me a wig!
  A wig, little pig!
  A pig in a wig!
Why, whoever before saw a pig in a wig!

Where are you going, you little pig?
Why, I'm going to the ball to dance a fine jig!
  A jig, little pig!
  A pig dance a jig!
Well, I never before saw a pig dance a jig!

Thomas Hood

13

The Fish in the Pond

Words by Michael Richmond, music by Nola York

The fish in the pond goes wriggling along,
When the fish goes swimming all the summer long.
Can you make your hands go wriggling along?
Just like the fish in the pond?

The wings on the bird go flapping up and down,
As the bird goes flying high above the town,
Can you make your hands go flapping up and down?
Just like the wings of the bird?

The wheels on the bus go round and round and
    round,
As they travel over miles and miles of ground.
Can you make your hands go round and round and
    round?
Just like the wheels on the bus?

I Wonder

I wonder if elephants ever catch colds?
If kangaroos ever get coughs?
Do spiders and snakes ever shiver and sneeze?
Can pandas and panthers catch a disease?
I wonder if elephants ever catch colds,
And if kangaroos ever get coughs?

Anne West

Follow My Leader

Words and music by Jenyth Worsley
Music arranged by Nola York

flea went hop-ping hop-ping hop-ping,

Ov-er the field where the grass— is green.

On his way he met a grass-hop-per —

Won't you fol-low my lea-der with me?

A flea went hopping, hopping, hopping,
Over the field where the grass is green.
On his way he met a grasshopper —
Won't you follow my leader with me?

A grasshopper went hopping, hopping,
Over the field where the grass is green
On his way he met a little frog —
Won't you follow my leader with me?

A frog went hopping, hopping, hopping,
Over the field where the grass is green,
On his way he met a rabbit —
Won't you follow my leader with me?

A rabbit went hopping, hopping, hopping,
Over the field where the grass is green.
On his way we heard him calling —
Won't you follow my leader with me?

All of us go hopping, hopping, hopping,
Rabbit and grasshopper, frog and flea.
If you'd like to come and play with us —
Won't you follow my leader with me?

The Bee Goes Buzzing

The bee goes buzzing round the flower — bzz, bzz,
The bee goes buzzing round the flower — bzz, bzz.
The bee goes buzzing round hour after hour,
The bee goes buzzing round the flower.

The bee makes honey in the hive — bzz, bzz,
The bee makes honey in the hive — bzz, bzz,
When the honey's ready, the beekeeper arrives,
The bee makes honey in the hive.

So let's say thank you to the bee — bzz, bzz,
Let's say thank you to the bee — bzz, bzz,
For the honey that we spread on our bread for tea,
Let's say thank you to the bee — bzz, bzz, bzzzzzz

Tony Aitken

Teddybear, Teddybear

Teddybear, teddybear, turn around,
Teddybear, teddybear, touch the ground.
Teddybear, teddybear, touch your nose,
Teddybear, teddybear, touch your toes.

Traditional

We're Going on a Bearhunt

This version written and arranged by Alison McMorland

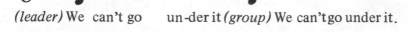

One person leads the others, who copy everything he does in words and actions

Chorus

Sing	We're going on a bearhunt. *(leader)*
	We're going on a bearhunt. (group)
	We're going to catch a big one.
	We're going to catch a big one.
Say	I'm not scared.
	I'm not scared.
	What a beautiful day.
	What a beautiful day.
	Oh! Oh!
	Oh! Oh!
Say	GRASS!
	Grass!
	Long, wavy grass.
	Long, wavy grass.
Sing	We can't go over it.
	We can't go over it.
	We can't go under it.
	We can't go under it.
Say	We'll have to go THROUGH IT! *(all)*
	Ssh! Ssh! Ssh! Ssh!
	Ssh! Ssh! Ssh! Ssh!

Chorus

Say	TREES! *(group repeat)*
	Big, tall trees. *(group repeat)*
Sing	We can't go over it . . .
Say	We'll have to go THROUGH IT! *(all)*

Click! Click! Click! Click!
Click! Click! Click! Click!

Chorus

Say   MUD! *(group repeat)*
              Thick, squelchy mud. *(group repeat)*
Sing   We can't go over it . . .
Say   We'll have to go THROUGH IT! *(all)*
              Slurp! Slurp! Slurp! Slurp!
              Slurp! Slurp! Slurp! Slurp!

Chorus (first six lines) then:

Say   Oh! Oh!
              Oh! Oh!
Sing   Two black furry ears.
              Two black furry ears.
              One black wet nose.
              One black wet nose.
              Two sharp pointed teeth.
              Two sharp pointed teeth.
Say   It's a Bear!
              It's a Bear!
              Quick! Run back *(leader only)*
              Throughout the mud — Slurp! Slurp!
              Slurp! Slurp!
              Through the trees — Click! Click! Click!
              Click!
              Through the grass — Ssh! Ssh! Ssh! Ssh!
              Quick back home and slam the door!

21

Donkey, Donkey

Donkey, Donkey,
Old and grey
Open your mouth
And gently bray.
Lift your ears
And blow your horn.
To wake the world,
This sleepy morn.

Traditional

Hey, Diddle Diddle

Hey, diddle diddle, the cat and the fiddle,
The cow jumped over the moon;
The little dog laughed to see such fun,
And the dish ran away with the spoon.

Traditional

Rat-a-tat-tat

Child and adult take alternate lines,
beginning with the child

Rat-a-tat-tat!
Who is that?
Only Grandma's pussy cat
What do you want?
A pint of milk.
Where's your money?
In my pocket.
Where's your pocket?
I forgot it

Rat-a-tat-tat!
Who is there?
Only a little teddybear.
What do you want?
A dish of honey.
Where's your money?
In my jacket.
Where's your jacket?
Didn't pack it.

First verse traditional
second verse by Mary Haydon

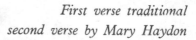

Walking in the Jungle

Walking in the jungle,
What do I see?
Roar, roar, roar!
A big lion roaring,
At me, me, me!

Make up your own verses
using different animals and noises

Traditional

Caspar the Cat

Caspar the cat,
Lives in a flat,
And he hates to get his fur soggy.
 Pretend to be a cat and miaow crossly
When he's caught in a shower,
He turns very sour,
And then he's a bad-tempered moggy!
 Miaow very crossly and pretend to shake water off

Valerie McCarthy

Donkey Riding

Were you ever in Quebec,
Stowing timbers on a deck,
Where there's a king in his golden crown
   Riding on a donkey?

Hey ho, and away we go,
   Donkey riding, donkey riding,
Hey ho, and away we go,
   Riding on a donkey.

Were you ever in Cardiff Bay,
Where the folks all shout, Hooray!
Here comes Johnnie with his three months' pay,
Riding on a donkey?

Hey ho, and away we go,
   Donkey riding, donkey riding,
Hey ho, and away we go,
   Riding on a donkey.

Were you ever off Cape Horn,
Where it's always fine and warm?
See the lion and the unicorn
   Riding on a donkey.

Hey ho, and away we go,
   Donkey riding, donkey riding,
Hey ho, and away we go,
   Riding on a donkey.

Traditional

The Hippopotamus Lullabye

Words and music by Nola York

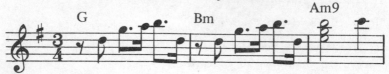

The hip-po-pot - a -mus

closed his eyes Slow - ly

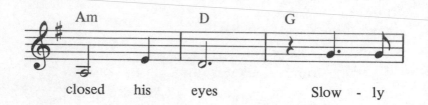

yawned__ and heaved a big sigh. ___ He

fell___ a - sleep___ in a big mud

pie While his mom - ma sang him a

lull - a - bye_____ She sang

Chorus

oh - oh - oh - oh - oh - oh - oh - oh -

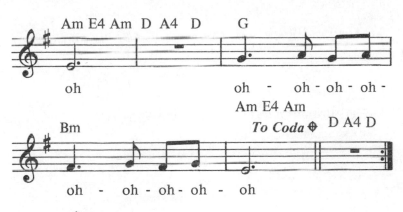

oh oh - oh - oh - oh -

oh - oh - oh - oh - oh

oh - oh - oh - oh.

Rall.

27

The hippopotamus closed his eyes,
Slowly yawned and heaved a big sigh.
He fell asleep in a great mud pie
While his momma sang him a lullabye.

Chorus
She sang: 'Oh, oh, oh, oh, oh, oh, oh, oh, oh,
oh, oh, oh, oh, oh, oh, oh, oh; oh, oh, oh, oh.

He dreamt he joined a circus act;
Danced and juggled like an acrobat,
Turning cartwheels in the sky
While his momma sang him a lullabye.

Chorus

Pretty music the band all played
As the hippopotamus joined the parade,
And in his dreams he went flying high
While his momma sang him a lullabye.

Chorus

The Ants Go Marching

This version written and arranged by Alison McMorland

The ants go march-ing one by one, Hur-rah, hur-

rah,___ The ants go march-ing one by one, Hur-

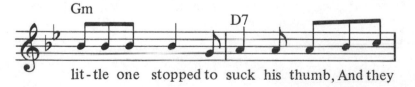

rah,___ hur-rah,___ The ants go marching one by one, The

lit-tle one stopped to suck his thumb, And they

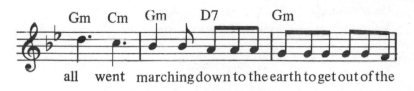

all went marching down to the earth to get out of the

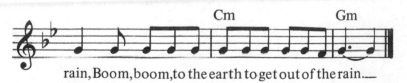

rain, Boom, boom, to the earth to get out of the rain.___

The ants go marching one by one,
Hurrah, hurrah.
The ants go marching one by one,
Hurrah, hurrah.
The ants go marching one by one,
The little one stopped to suck his thumb,
And they all went marching down
To the earth to get out of the rain,
Boom, boom,
To the earth to get out of the rain.

The ants go marching two by two . . .
The little one stopped to do up his shoe

The ants go marching three by three . . .
The little one stopped to climb a tree

The ants go marching four by four . . .
The little one stopped to knock at the door

The ants go marching five by five . . .
The little one stopped to learn to drive

The ants go marching six by six . . .
The little one stopped to pick up sticks

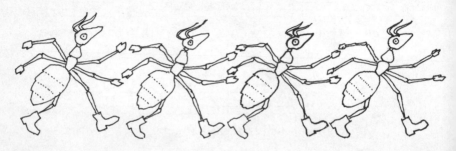

The ants go marching seven by seven . . .
The little one stopped and went to heaven

The ants go marching eight by eight . . .
The little one stopped to shut the gate

The ants go marching nine by nine . . .
The little one stopped to walk a line

The ants go marching ten by ten . . .
The little one stopped to say THE END.

Choosing a Pet

A cat or dog or a mouse in the house?
A hamster, a budgie, or a bird?
Don't choose a croc,
It'd give mum a shock,
If it sat in the bath and it purred.

You could have a frog or a gentle old toad,
A lizard, a goldfish or two.
But take my advice —
It wouldn't be nice,
To ask for a red kangaroo!

Gladys Whitred

Did You Ever?

Traditional words and music

Did you ev-er, ever, ever, ever, ev-er,— Did you

ev - er see a mouse paint a house? No, I

nev-er, nev-er, nev-er, nev-er, nev-er,— No, I

nev - er saw a mouse paint a house.

Did you ever, ever, ever,
Did you ever see a mouse paint a house?
No, I never, never, never, never,
No, I never saw a mouse paint a house!

Did you ever see a pig dance a jig?

Did you ever see a crow shovel snow?

Did you ever see a snake bake a cake?

Did you ever see a fish wash a dish?

Did you ever see a goat sail a boat?

Did you ever see a snail wave his tail?

Did you ever see a cat wear a hat?

Samantha the Panther

Words by Michael Richmond, music by Nola York

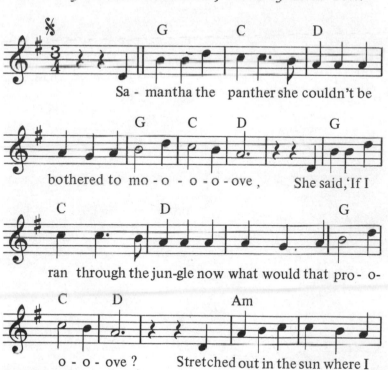

Sa - mantha the panther she couldn't be bothered to mo - o - o - o - ove , She said, 'If I ran through the jun-gle now what would that pro - o - o - o - ove ? Stretched out in the sun where I

am I can peace-fully la - a - aze, I
can't think of an - y way bet-ter for pass-ing the
da - a - a - a - a - ays. She asked a green bird who replied with a glance, 'Itwas Monday I know when I
flew over France, 'It's Thursday tomorrow now leave me in
peace. I promised my friends I would meet them in
Gree - ee - ee - ee-ee-eece.'

Samantha the Panther she couldn't be bothered to
   move,
She said, 'If I ran through the jungle now what
   would that prove?
Stretched out in the sun where I am I can peacefully
   laze,
I can't think of any way better for passing the days.'

She asked a green bird who replied with a glance,
'It was Monday I know when I flew over France,
It's Thursday tomorrow; now leave me in peace.
I promised my friends I would meet them in
   Greece.'

Samantha the Panther was having a beautiful dream
She dreamt of a party and cakes that were covered in
   cream
And then she woke up with a jump and she said,
   'Goodness me
My birthday's on Thursday, I wonder what day this
   can be.'

Samantha the Panther was pleased she had found
   out at last
How awful if she hadn't known till her birthday had
   passed.
So after a long drink of milk from a coconut cup
She went back to sleep — it was Saturday when she
   woke up.

Great Big Wonderful Worm

Words and music by Tony Aitken

Oh, I'm a great big won-der-ful worm, I am_____ Yes, I'm a great big won-der-ful worm, I am_____ I can ride a horse and I can drive a car; I can ride a space-ship all the way to

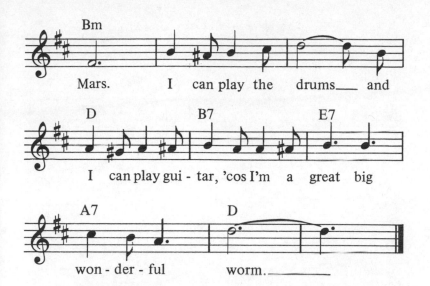

Oh, I'm a great big wonderful worm, I am —
Yes, I'm a great big wonderful worm, I am.
I can ride a horse and I can drive a car;
I can ride a space-ship all the way to Mars.
I can play the drums, and I can play guitar,
'Cos I'm a great big wonderful worm.

This Little Piggy

Wiggle each toe in turn

This little piggy went to market,
This little piggy stayed at home,
This little piggy had roast beef,
This little piggy had none,
And this little piggy went wee, wee, wee —
All the way home.

Traditional

All the Ducks

Traditional, music arranged by Tony Aitken

All the ducks are swimming in the water Fol-de-rid-dle I doh, fol-de-rid-dle I doh, All the ducks are swimming in the water, Fol dee fol-de-rid-dle dee.

All the ducks are swimming in the water,
Fol-de-riddle-I-doh, fol-de-riddle-I-doh,
All the ducks are swimming in the water,
Fol-dee-fol-de-riddle-dee.

The bridge is broken — however shall we mend it?
Doo-wacker, doo-wacker; doo-wacker-do-wacker.
Doo-wacker, doo-wacker-do.

In my boat I'll gladly row you over
Shalla-wally-doo-wap; shalla-wally-doo-wap
Doo-wap, shalla-wally-doo.

Three new pennies I will gladly pay you.
Ting-a-ling-a-ding-dong; ting-a-ling-a-ding-dong.
Ting-ling-tinga-ling-a-ding.

My Teddybear

He's rather old,
And he looks a bit grubby;
He's not very tall,
And he's ever so chubby.
His right ear is bent,
His paw has a tear;
His smile is lopsided,
But I don't really care.
I'll love him for ever,
'Cos he's my teddybear.

Valerie McCarthy

Ten little Witch-cats

A counting rhyme for Hallowe'en

TEN little witch-cats flying in a line;
One fell from the broomstick — miaow —
so then there were nine.

NINE little witch-cats flying out late;
One fell fast asleep — miaow —
so then there were eight.

EIGHT little witch-cats flying up to heaven;
One landed on the moon — miaow —
so then there were seven.

SEVEN little witch-cats trying magic tricks;
One said the wrong spell — miaow —
so then there were six.

SIX little witch-cats playing round the witch's hive;
One was chased by a bumblebee — miaow —
so then there were five.

FIVE little witch-cats sitting at the witch's door;
One strayed inside — miaow —
so then there were four.

FOUR little witch-cats wondering what to be;
One became a show cat — miaow —
so then there were three.

THREE little witch-cats walking round the zoo;
One was swallowed by a fish — miaow —
so then there were two.

TWO little witch-cats going for a run;
One was frightened by a dog — miaow —
so then there was one.

ONE little witch-cat, missing all the others,
Wished a magic wish — miaow —
and home came his brothers!

Elizabeth Barrowcliffe

One, Two, Three, Four, Five

One, two, three, four, five,
Once I caught a fish alive,
Six, seven, eight nine, ten,
Then I let it go again.
Why did you let it go?
Because it bit my finger so.
Which finger did it bite?
The little finger on the right.

Traditional

Things
We Do

Let's Go to the Moon

Let's go to the moon, shall we?
Let's go to the moon.
We'll build ourselves a little rocket ship,
So let's go to the moon, shall we?
Let's go to the moon.

Let's go to the moon, shall we?
Let's go to the moon.
And as we fly so high above the trees,
We'll see if the moon is really made of cheese.
So let's go to the moon, shall we?
Let's go to the moon.

Let's go to the moon, shall we?
Let's go to the moon.
And if a little moon-man we should see,
We'll knock at his door and ask him home for tea.
Oh, let's go to the moon, shall we?
Let's go to the moon.

Mari Griffiths

Girls and Boys Come Out to Play

Traditional words and music

Girls and boys, come out to play, The moon doth shine as

bright as day; Leave your sup-per and leave your sleep,

Come join your playfel-lows in the street.

Come with a whoop, and come with a call,

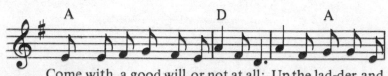

Come with a good will, or not at all; Up the lad-der and

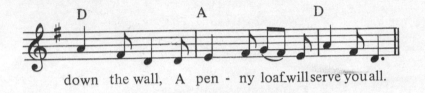

down the wall, A pen - ny loaf will serve you all.

Girls and boys come out to play,
The moon doth shine as bright as day;
Leave your supper and leave your sleep,
Come join your playfellows in the street.

Come with a whoop, and come with a call,
Come with a good will or not at all;
Up the ladder and down the wall,
A penny loaf will serve you all.

The Mitten Song

'Thumbs in the thumb-place,
Fingers all together!'
This is the song
We sing in mitten-weather.
When it is cold,
It doesn't matter whether
Mittens are wool,
Or made of finest leather.
This is the song
We sing in mitten-weather:
'Thumbs in the thumb-place,
Fingers all together!'

Marie Louise Allen

Stamping

Stamp your feet,
Stamp your feet,
Put them each one in a shoe,
Count them very carefully,
How many are there?
Two!

Sniff with your nose,
Sniff with your nose,
Have a lot of fun,
How many noses have you got?
I think the answer's . . .
One!

Blink your eyes,
Blink your eyes,
Are they brown or blue?
Whether they're brown or whether they're blue,
I bet you've got just —
Two!

Nod your head,
Nod your head,
Put it in the sun.
I'd be surprised if you've got more heads,
Than me — and I've got . . .
One!

Wriggle your fingers,
Wriggle your fingers,
Make them come alive.
If you count your fingers you will
Find that there are . . .
Five!

David Bell

Washing Line

I didn't know my shirt could dance,
Until I took a look by chance,
And saw that clever shirt of mine
Was dancing on the washing line.
It flipped and flapped and flopped
And when the wind dropped, it stopped.

My socks were up there dancing too
And leaping like a kangaroo.
They kicked up high, they kicked out wide
As if my feet were still inside.
They flipped and flapped and flopped.
And when the wind dropped, they stopped.

My handkerchief began to wave,
That's quite a new way to behave,
So I joined in and danced with glee.
My shirt, socks, handkerchief — and me.
We flipped and flapped and flopped.
And when the wind dropped, we stopped.

Michael Richmond

I Am Mixing Colours

Words by Michael Richmond, music by Nola York

I am mix-ing colours, mix-ing colours, mix-ing colours, I am mixing colours from my new paint box.

Take some yel-low and then add,

Blue as bright as bright can be —

Mix to - geth - er on my pad

Blue and yel-low turn to green, you see.

I am mixing colours, mixing colours, mixing colours,
I am mixing colours from my new paint box.

Take some yellow and then add
Blue as bright as can be —
Mix together on my pad,
Blue and yellow turn to green — you see.

I am mixing colours, etc.

Let me take some yellow now,
Then I'll have a dab of red
Now it's changed, I don't know how —
Yellow and red make orange instead.

I am mixing colours, etc.

Now I'll take a spot more red
An mix it up with . . . white, I think.
Red mixed up with white I said
Have turned into a blushing pink!

Round and Round the Garden

Round and round the garden
Like a teddybear,
One step,
Two steps,
Tickle you under there.

Traditional

51

In My Little Bed

Traditional, music arranged by Christopher Rowe

There's a fox in a box in my lit-tle bed,

My lit-tle bed, my lit-tle bed, There's a

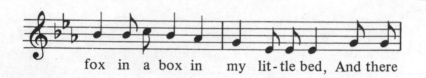

fox in a box in my lit-tle bed, And there

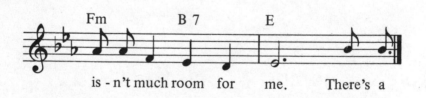

is-n't much room for me. There's a

There's a fox in a box in my little bed,
My little bed, my little bed,
There's a fox in a box in my little bed,
And there isn't much room for me.

There's a goat in a coat in my little bed . . .

There's a snake in a cake in my little bed . . .

There's a pup in a cup in my little bed . . .

There's a lamb in some jam in my little bed . . .

There's a mouse in a house in my little bed . . .

There's a bear in a chair in my little bed . . .

Collecting

Do you like collecting?
Do you like collecting things?
Coloured beads, bits of wood;
Shiny pebbles, knotted strings?
Have you got a box of treasures?
Full of most important stuff?
Some bottle tops, an old tape measure,
Last year's conkers, brown and tough?
A toothless comb of yellow plastic,
Some stretchy sort of red elastic?
A broken car, an old jam jar,
A postcard from a friend?
Do you like collecting?
Do you like collecting things?

Tony Aitken

These Boots Are Made For Walking

Words and music by Tony Aitken

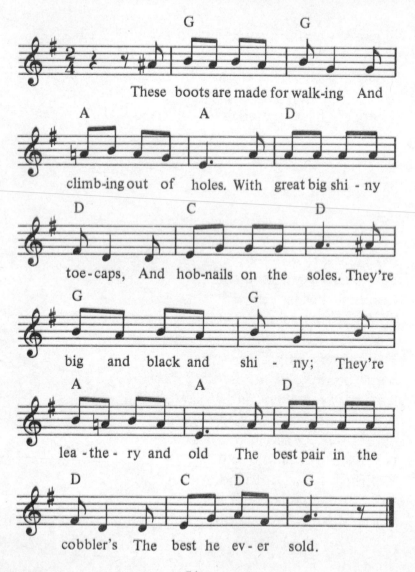

These boots are made for walk-ing And
climb-ing out of holes. With great big shi - ny
toe - caps, And hob-nails on the soles. They're
big and black and shi - ny; They're
lea - the - ry and old The best pair in the
cobbler's The best he ev - er sold.

These boots are made for walking
And climbing out of holes.
With great big shiny toecaps,
And hobnails on the soles.
They're big and black and shiny;
They're leathery and old
The best pair in the cobbler's
The best he ever sold.

When climbing up a mountain;
Walking down the street;
Marching round the fountain,
With my best friends on my feet.
They're big and black and shiny,
They're leathery and old,
The best pair in the cobbler's;
The best he ever sold.

Repeat last two lines to finish

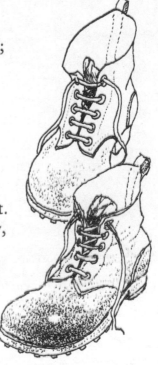

Box of Sounds

Turn the key,
Turn the key,
Turn the key round —
Open the box,
And wait for the sound . . . . .   *Jenyth Worsley*

This rhyme was a great favourite on 'Listen with Mother'.
Children can make their own sound effects, animal noises, etc.
for parents to guess

Tearing Paper

Words by Michael Richmond, music by Nola York

I like tear-ing pa - per,

Tear -ing pa-per is a whole lot of fun. I like

tear-ing pa - per. What shall we do when the

pa-per tear-ing's done? Tearing Tearing tissue paper,

White and crink-ly tis-sue pa- per. Hold the pieces,

let them go . Tis -sue pa-per looks like snow.

I like tearing paper,
Paper tearing is a whole lot of fun.
I like tearing paper,
What shall we do when
The paper tearing's done?

Tearing, tearing tissue paper,
White and crinkly tissue paper.
Hold the pieces, let them go.
Tissue paper looks like snow.

Tearing, tearing wrapping paper,
Brown and crackly wrapping paper.
Hold the pieces, drop them all.
Then they're autumn leaves that fall.

Tearing, tearing silver paper,
Shiny, shiny silver paper.
Drop the pieces from the sky,
And they rain out of the sky.

If I Had Wings

If I had wings, feathers and things
I'd have a go at flying.
I'd find a hill somewhere about,
Flap my wings, and with a shout,
I'd soar into the air.
If there was lots of time to spare
I'd soon get used to being there!
I'd say hello, and join the crowd
Of birds behind the nearest cloud;
And as I flew down without a sound
I'd surprise the people on the ground.
As I learned to fly with ease,
I'd find my friends and then I'd tease
Them flying all around their gardens
Saying 'I beg your pardon . . .
But leave your scooter and your trike,
Forget your go-cart and your bike —
Just grow some wings, feathers and things
And have a go at flying!'

Tony Aitken

I Know a Little House

I know a little house,
With walls, one, two, three, four;
Draw four walls in the air with your finger
With ivy climbing up them,
Wiggle fingers up and down
And roses round the door.
Put the tips of your fingers over your
head to make an arch
It's got four little windows
With shutters open wide
Pretend to open shutters
And a lovely windy staircase,
That goes up and up inside.
Wind hand round and round
There's a roof with a crooked chimney,
Make a roof with your hands and bend
one finger
And in the garden a tree so tall,
Spread your arms out and stand on tiptoe
That if you were to climb it,
You'd see over the garden wall.
Stand on tiptoe and pretend to peep
over wall
                                    Valerie McCarthy

That's How the Garden Grows

Words and music by David Bell

VERSE

My mum likes to wa-ter the flowers,
Wa-ter the flowers, wa-ter the flowers;
My mum likes to wa-ter the flowers,—
That's how the gar-den grows.

CHORUS

Sun shine, Rain fall, wind blow. Cut grass, wa-ter flowers, dig up the weeds—That's how the gar-den grows.

My mum likes to water the flowers,
Water the flowers, water the flowers;
My mum likes to water the flowers —
That's how the garden grows.

Chorus
Sun shine,
Rain fall, wind blow.
Cut grass, water flowers, dig up the weeds —
That's how the garden grows.

My dad likes to cut down the grass,
Cut down the grass, cut down the grass;
My dad likes to cut down the grass —
That's how the garden grows.

Chorus

I just get to dig up the weeds,
Dig up the weeds, dig up the weeds;
All I do is dig up the weeds —
That's how the garden grows.

Chorus

I'm Looking in My Mirror

I'm looking in my mirror,
Do you know what I can see?
A face — with two round eyes,
It looks a lot like me!

I'm looking in my mirror,
Do you know what I can see?
A face — with two round eyes,
And two ears on the side,
It looks a lot like me!

I'm looking in my mirror,
Do you know what I can see?
A face — with two round eyes,
And two ears on the side,
And a nose in the middle —
I can make it wriggle,
It looks a lot like me!

I'm looking in my mirror,
Do you know what I can see?
A face — with two round eyes,
And two ears on the side,
A nose in the middle —
I can make it wriggle,
And a smile underneath —
That's my mouth and my teeth.
It looks a lot like me!

Tony Aitken

The Swinging Song

Swing, swang, swung, swong,
Listen to my swinging song.
Nose, knees, ears, toes,
Elephants have all of those.
So have you and so have I,
But none of us can fly.

Swing, swang, swung, swong,
Listen to my swinging song.
Nose, knees, ears, toes,
Do you think, do you suppose,
An elephant would want to fly?
Well, he could always try.

Swing, swang, swung, swong,
Listen to my swinging song.
Nose, knees, ears, toes,
On my swing, if I chose,
I could very nearly fly,
Swinging low and swinging high.
Swing, swang, swung, swong,
Listen to my swinging song.

Rachel Birley

I Have a Bonnet
Trimmed With Blue

Traditional, music arranged by Alison McMorland

I have a bonnet trimmed with blue. Do you wear it?

Yes, I do. When I go to meet my John,

Then I put my bonnet on, Bon-net on,

bon-net on, Then I put my bon-net on.

I have a bonnet trimmed with blue.
Do you wear it? Yes, I do.
When I go to meet my John,
Then I put my bonnet on.
    Bonnet on, bonnet on;
    Then I put my bonnet on.

I have a skirt all trimmed with green,
The prettiest one that's ever seen.
And I wear it when I can
Going to the fair with my young man.
  My young man, my young man;
   Going to the fair with my young man.

I have a mantle trimmed with brown,
The bonniest one that's in the town.
And I wear it when I can.
Going to the fair with my young man.
  My young man, my young man;
   Going to the fair with my young man.

My young man has gone to sea,
When he comes back he'll marry me.
He buys biscuits, I buy tarts,
Don't you think we're jolly sweethearts.
  Jolly sweethearts, jolly sweethearts,
   Don't you think we're jolly sweethearts.

We'll All
Have Tea

Polly Put the Kettle On

Polly put the kettle on,
Polly put the kettle on,
Polly put the kettle on,
We'll all have tea.

Sukey take it off again,
Sukey take it off again,
Sukey take it off again,
They've all gone away.

Traditional

Jelly on Your Plate

Jelly on your plate,
Jelly on your plate,
Wibble, wobble,
Jelly on your plate.

Jelly in your spoon,
Jelly in your spoon,
Wibble, wobble,
Jelly in your spoon.

Jelly in your tum,
Jelly in your tum,
Wibble, wobble,
Jelly in your tum.

First verse anon,
additional verses by Gladys Whitred

Walking in the Garden

Words by Michael Richmond, music by Nola York

I'm walking in the garden Where the vegetables are

grow-ing and as I go I'll let you know ex-

act-ly where I'm go -ing

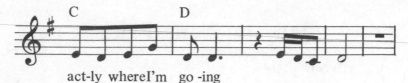

Once a-round the rad-ish-es, In and out the tur-nips.

Straight past the cab-bag-es And home a - gain I'm

I'm walking in the garden
Where the vegetables are growing,
And as I walk I'll let you know
Exactly where I'm going.

Once around the radishes,
In and out the turnips.
Straight past the cabbages
And home again.

I'm walking in the garden
Where the fruit is busy growing,
And as I walk I'll let you know
Exactly where I'm going.

Once around the apple tree,
In and out the cherries;
Straight past the strawberries,
And home again.

I'm walking in the garden
Where the flowers are all growing,
And as I walk I'll let you know
Exactly where I'm going.

Once around the marigolds,
In and out the roses;
Straight past the clover patch
And home again.

Ten Fat Sausages

Ten fat sausages sitting in a pan;
One went 'POP!' and another went 'BANG!'
  All clap hands

Apples

Apples hanging way up high;
Reach up, reach up.
  Stretch arm up
Apples hanging way up high —
Soon they'll be an apple pie
Reach up, reach up.

Apples peeled and apples cored;
Slice up, slice up.
  Pretend to slice
Apples peeled and apples cored
Apple pie with custard poured.
  Pretend to pour custard
Slice up, slice up.

Apples in an apple pie;
Eat up, eat up,
  Pretend to eat
Apples in an apple pie,
Once were hanging way up high.
Eat up, eat up.

Michael Richmond

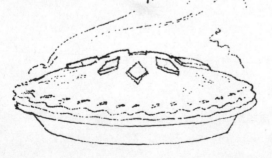

Pop Goes the Weasel

Half a pound of tuppenny rice,
Half a pound of treacle,
That's the way the money goes;
Pop goes the weasel.

Up and down the City Road,
In and out the Eagle,
That's the way the money goes,
Pop goes the weasel.

Traditional

Currant Buns

Five currant buns in a baker's shop,
Round and fat with sugar on the top.
Along came a boy with a penny one day,
Bought a currant bun and took it away.

Four currant buns, etc.

Traditional

Pat-a-Cake

Pat-a-cake, pat-a-cake,
Baker's man,
Make me a cake as fast as you can.
Pack it and prick it and mark it with B;
And put it in the oven for Baby and me.

Traditional

Hippety-hop to the Candy Shop

Hippety-hop to the candy shop,
To buy a stick of candy;
One for you,
One for me,
And one for sister Sandy.

Traditional

Little Miss Muffett

Little Miss Muffett
Sat on her tuffet
Eating her curds and whey.
Along came a spider
And sat down beside her
And frightened Miss Muffett away!

Traditional

I Had a Little Nut Tree

I had a little nut tree,
Nothing would it bear,
But a silver nutmeg,
And a golden pear.
The king of Spain's daughter
Came to visit me,
And all for the sake of my little nut tree.
I skipped over water,
I skipped over sea,
And all the birds in the air
Couldn't catch me.

Traditional

75

Those
Funny People

The Grand Old Duke of York

Oh, the grand old Duke of York
He had ten thousand men,
He marched them up to the top of the hill,
And he marched them down again.

And when they were up, they were up,
And when they were down, they were down,
And when they were only half way up,
They were neither up nor down.

Traditional

Two Old Gentlemen

A finger play

Two old gentlemen met in the lane,
Bowed most politely,
    Wriggle thumbs
Bowed once again,
How do you do?
How do you do?
And how do you do again?

Two thin ladies . . . (*forefingers*)
Two tall policemen . . . (*middle fingers*)
Two naughty schoolboys . . . (*fourth fingers*)
Two little babies . . . (*little fingers*)

Traditional

Charlotte's Navy Blue Shoes

Words and music by Nola York

Char-lotte's got new na - vy blue shoes._

She loves to dance in her na-vy blue shoes._

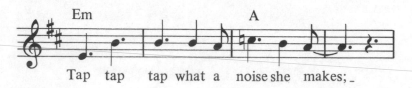

Tap tap tap what a noise she makes;_

Stamp stamp stamp all ov - er the place.

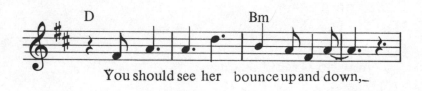

You should see her bounce up and down,_

The way she turns a-round and a - round.

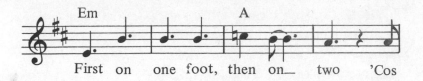

First on one foot, then on_ two 'Cos

Char-lotte's got new na - vy blue shoes.

Do do n do do_ do do n do do_

do do n do do_ wou wou wou.

Charlotte's got new navy blue shoes.
She loves to dance in her navy blue shoes.
Tap-tap-tap what a noise she makes;
Stamp-stamp-stamp all over the place.
You should see her bounce up and down,
The way she twirls around and around.
First on one foot, then on two —
'Cos Charlotte's got new navy blue shoes.

Charlotte's got new navy blue shoes.
She loves to dance in her navy blue shoes.
Slap-slap-slap on the kitchen floor;
Sliding down by the garden wall.
Matthew the dog starts twitching his toes,
Tapping feet are getting far too close.
Hide away, that's the thing to do —
'Cos Charlotte's got new navy blue shoes.

Funny Jim

Words and music by Christopher Rowe

I know a fun-ny man called Jim, And
I am ve-ry, ve-ry fond of him. He
wears his shoes up - on his head And
rides a bi-cy-cle in bed.

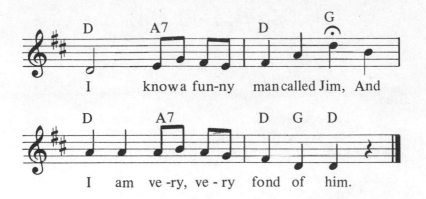

I know a funny man called Jim,
And I am very, very fond of him.
He wears his shoes upon his head
And rides a bicycle to bed.
I know a funny man called Jim,
And I am very, very fond of him.

I know a silly man called Joe
Who likes his weeds to grow and grow.
He will dig for hours and hours
And take up all his lovely flowers.
I know a silly man called Joe
Who likes his weeds to grow and grow.

I know a nosy man called John
Who has to know whatever's going on.
What you say, what you do,
Nosy John is watching YOU.
I know a nosy man called John
Who has to know whatever's going on.

The Bold, Bad Pirate

A joining-in game

Adult The pirate's big,
The pirate's fat
He wears black boots,
And a great big hat,
When he speaks,
His voice is low,
What does the pirate say?

Child YO HO HO!

Adult The pirate's bad,
The pirate's bold,
He sails the seas,
Stealing silver and gold,
He's the wickedest man,
You'll ever know,
What does the pirate say?

Child YO HO HO!

Adult I'm ever so big
And I'm ever so fat,
I wear black boots,
And a great big hat,
When I speak,
My voice is low,
I'm a bold, bad pirate —

Child YO HO HO!

Adult   I'm ever so bad,
And I'm ever so bold,
I sail the seas,
Stealing silver and gold,
I'm the wickedest man,
You'll ever know,
I'm a bold, bad pirate,
Child   YO HO HO!

David Bell

Mary, Mary

Mary, Mary,
Quite contrary,
How does your garden grow?
With silver bells,
And cockleshells,
And pretty maids all in a row.

Traditional

Jack and Jill

Jack and Jill went up the hill
To fetch a pail of water.
Jack fell down and broke his crown,
And Jill came tumbling after.

Traditional

The Fair-haired Baby Boy

I know a fair-haired baby boy,
His loving mother's pride and joy,
He fills the house with playful song,
Until, that is,
He does something wrong:
Then it's:
Pots of paint upset on the floor,
Pictures of monsters carved on the door,
Cupboard door open,
Clothes thrown about,
Cat left in when it should have been out . . .
Because:
When he's good, he's very, very good —
And when he's bad, he's awful!

Tony Aitken

The Blue-eyed Baby Girl

I know a blue-eyed baby girl,
With a winning smile and a little kiss curl,
She fills the house with playful song,
Until, that is,
She does something wrong:
Then it's:
Holding her breath 'til her face goes red,
Flatly refusing to go to bed,
Mud in her shoes,
Jam in hair,
Yet at times you'd hardly know she was there —
Because:
When she's good, she's very, very good —
And when she's bad, she's awful!

Tony Aitken

Michael Finnigin

Traditional words and music

1. There was an old man called Mi-chael Finnigin,

He grew whis-kers on his chin-i-gin, The

wind came up and blew them in-i-gin, Poor old Mi-chael

Fin-ni-gin. Be-gin-i-gin! There Fin-ni-gin. STOP!

There was an old man called Michael Finnigin,
He grew whiskers on his chinigin,
The wind came up and blew them inigin,
  Poor old Michael Finnigin. Beginigin!

88

There was an old man called Michael Finnigin,
He kicked up an awful dinigin,
Because they said he must not singigin,
   Poor old Michael Finnigin. Beginigin!

There was an old man called Michael Finnigin,
He went fishing with a pinigin,
Caught a fish but dropped it inigin,
   Poor old Michael Finnigin. Beginigin!

There was an old man called Michael Finnigin,
Climbed a tree and barked his shinigin,
Took off several yards of skinigin,
   Poor old Michael Finnigin. Beginigin!

There was an old man called Michael Finnigin,
He grew fat and then grew thinigin,
Then he died and had to beginigin,
   Poor old Michael Finnigin, STOP!

Lucy Locket

Lucy Locket lost her pocket
Kitty Fisher found it
There was not a penny in it,
But a ribbon round it.

Traditional

Hush-a-Bye, Baby

Traditional words and music

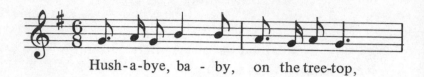

Hush-a-bye, ba - by, on the tree-top,

When the wind blows the cra - dle will rock;

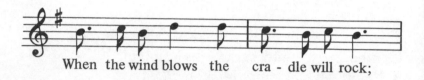

When the bough breaks the cra - dle will fall,

Down— comes ba - by, cra - dle and all.

Hush-a-bye, baby on the tree top,
When the wind blows the cradle will rock.
When the bough breaks the cradle will fall,
Down will come baby, cradle and all.

The Funny Family

Traditional, music arranged by Alison McMorland

Once long a - go,___ there lived a fun - ny

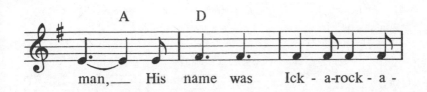

man,___ His name was Ick - a-rock - a -

ick - a-rock a - ran.___ His legs were

long and his feet were small,___ And he

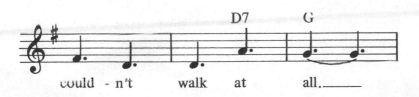

could - n't walk at all.___

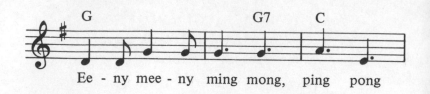

Ee - ny mee - ny ming mong, ping pong

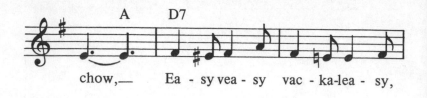

chow,— Ea - sy vea - sy vac - ka-lea - sy,

ea - sy vea - sy vow.— Ee - ny mee - ny

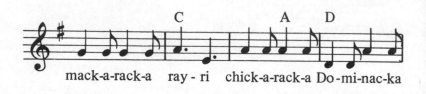

mack-a-rack-a ray - ri chick-a-rack-a Do -mi-nac-ka

lol - li - pop - pa, om pom push.—

Once long ago, there lived a funny man.
His name was Icka-rocka-icka-rocka-ran.
His legs were long and his feet were small,
   And he couldn't walk at all.

Eeny meeny ming mong, ping pong chow,
Easy veasy vacka-leasy, easy veasy vow.
Eeny meeny macka-racka, ray-ri chicka-racka
Dominacka, lollipoppa, om pom push.

He had a wife, did this funny man,
Her name was Iddy-tiddy-ran-tan-tan.
Her legs were long, and her feet were small,
 And she couldn't walk at all.

Chorus

They had children, one and two,
Chickity-cha and Chickity-choo.
Their legs were long and their feet were small,
 And they couldn't walk at all.

Chorus

Humpty Dumpty

Humpty Dumpty sat on a wall,
Humpty Dumpty had a great fall;
All the King's horses
And all the King's men,
Couldn't put Humpty together again.

Traditional

93

The Dingle-dangle Scarecrow

Traditional, music arranged by Alison McMorland

For lower voices, transpose to D, chords in brackets.

When all the cows were sleep - ing And the

sun had gone to bed, Up jumped the scare - crow, and

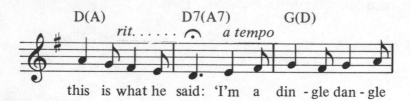

this is what he said: 'I'm a din - gle dan - gle

scare - crow With a flip - py flop - py hat, I

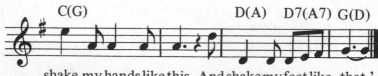

shake my hands like this, And shake my feet like that.'

When all the cows were sleeping
And the sun had gone to bed,
Up jumped the scarecrow,
And this is what he said:

'I'm a dingle-dangle scarecrow
With a flippy-floppy hat,
I can shake my hands like this,
And shake my feet like that.'

'I'm a dingle-dangle scarecrow
With a flippy-floppy hat,
I can shake my hands like this,
And shake my feet like that.'

When all the hens were roosting
And the moon behind a cloud,
Up jumped the scarecrow
And shouted very loud:

'I'm a dingle-dangle scarecrow,
With a flippy-floppy hat,
I can shake my arms like this,
And shake my feet like that.'

Dance, Thumbkin, Dance

Traditional words and music

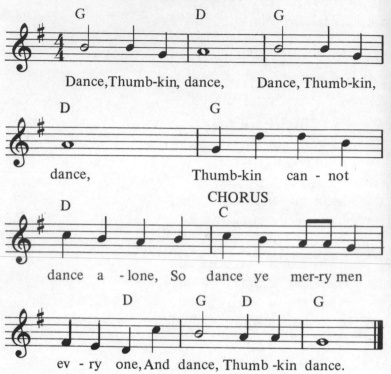

Dance, Thumb-kin, dance, Dance, Thumb-kin, dance, Thumb-kin can-not dance a-lone, So dance ye mer-ry men ev-ry one, And dance, Thumb-kin dance.

Dance, Thumbkin, dance,
Dance, Thumbkin, dance,
Thumbkin cannot dance alone,
So dance you merry men every one,
And dance, Thumbkin, dance.

Dance, Foreman, dance, etc.
Dance, Longman, dance, etc.
Dance, Ringman, dance, etc.